Other books by Noël Coward

Autobiography

Short Stories

Plays

Collected Plays

Novel

NOT YET THE DODO

and other verses

Noël Coward

NOT YET THE DODO

and other verses

Doubleday & Company, Inc.
Garden City, New York
1968

LIBRARY OF CONGRESS CATALOG CARD NUMBER 68–16885
COPYRIGHT © 1967 BY NOËL COWARD
ALL RIGHTS RESERVED
PRINTED IN THE UNITED STATES OF AMERICA
FIRST EDITION IN THE UNITED STATES OF AMERICA

FOR DIANA
with my love

CONTENTS

INTRODUCTION

Throughout most of the years of my life, since approximately nineteen hundred and eight, I have derived a considerable amount of private pleasure from writing verse. The impulse to arrange words in rhymes and rhythms must have been born in me. Although, as a matter of fact, I have long been aware that this particular impulse is in no way unique. It is an inherent instinct in the English character. It is surprising how many unexpected, non-literary minds take to verse at the slightest encouragement. In the Services for instance, particularly the Royal Navy, at least on the Bridges and in the Wardrooms where I have so frequently been a guest, the scribbling of doggerel to highlight some specific event or situation, is an accepted routine. There are few Admirals, Captains and Commanders who have not, at some time or other, dispatched rhymed couplets via their "Signals" operators to their opposite numbers in adjacent ships. In fact, verse and apt quotations from the Bible are sent whizzing back and forth as a matter of course. These are occasionally obscene, always pertinent and usually extremely witty. Whether or not the officers of other Navies indulge in this brain-teasing little game I do not know, but I doubt it, it is such a typically British brand of irreverent flippancy. In my own case I have automatically enjoyed verse as a means of gay communication with my intimates ever since I can remember. Lorn Loraine, my beloved secretary and English representative for forty-six years, is an expert at squeezing the maximum of business information and personal news into rhymed cables and telegrams which, together with my also rhymed replies, has afforded us both a lot of amusement. The amusement, however, is private and too esoteric to interest anyone apart from ourselves. Many of the communications exchanged would be completely unintelligible to the lay reader. The habit of doing it, however, has trained our inner ears to such an extent that we occasionally find it easier to correspond in rhyme than normally. All of which may help a little to explain why, at the age of sixty-six, I should suddenly publish a book of verse. True I did make the attempt many many years ago when I was no more than thirteen or fourteen. I managed to complete a book entitled *Vegetable Verse*, which was whimsical, arch and so self-consciously determined to be funny that I read it to-day with acute embarrassment. It was not, however, by any means devoid of talent; the words rhymed and the metres scanned and some isolated lines were not without a certain flair, and it is evident now that these embryonic effusions were early indications of my latent talent for writing lyrics. Oddly enough, although my adolescence was certainly actively precocious, I never made the mistake, even in my private mind, of imagining that I was a poet. To me poetry was then and still is in a different category altogether. Those dear old fairies at my christening in St. Alban's church, Teddington, Middlesex, endowed me with many rich gifts but a true poetic sense was not one of them. Perhaps with shrewd prescience of the sort of life I was destined to live, they realised that irony and humour would be more useful to me. By this I do not mean to imply that a sense of humour is necessarily a deterrent to genuine poetic impulse but I do feel that it can occasionally be a hindrance. The finer flights of lyric rapture can swiftly be blown off course by an irreverent gust of laughter and there are many lines written by major poets that I am unable to read without repressing a giggle. At any rate, in spite of my conviction that a true poetic sense has been denied me, I would like to point out, in fairness to myself, that here and there along the line I have written a phrase or two that are not entirely without grace. Having read poetry all my life for pleasure rather than from a sense of educational duty, my appreciation is naturally circumscribed by my personal tastes and prejudices. I admit that in my earlier years I did toil through certain turgid classics because I felt that doing so might help my development as a writer and, up to a point, I suppose it did.

I learned at least what, to me, was readable or unreadable, but after a very short while I gave up the struggle reflecting, perhaps with a tinge of sophistry, that my development as a writer would be more likely to be improved by reading what interested me than by reading what bored me to death.

Selecting the verses for this book which represent, I am stunned to realise, less than a quarter of my total output, has been an enjoyable and slightly nostalgic task. I found my mind continually being whisked away from the matter in hand by sudden sharp memories of where, when and in what circumstances many of them had been conceived and written. Nearly all of them I realised had originated in moving conveyances of various sorts; trains rushing across Continents, ships ploughing across Oceans, motorcars, riverboats, aeroplanes, rickshaws and on the backs of animals. I once churned out a few cheerful little couplets, riding on a camel in the Sahara desert which, so far as I can remember, were too obscene to be preserved for posterity. As however they happened to be blown away in a sandstorm they may after all be preserved for posterity and be discovered centuries hence like the Dead Sea Scrolls. As they were unsigned I hereby seize the opportunity of publicly disowning them.

NOT YET THE DODO

and other verses

P & O

The siren hoots three times its final warning
The first one long, the second two much shorter.
The passengers at the rail are suddenly stunned
Staring disconsolately at the Shanghai Bund
As the widening gulf of yellow river water
Between the ship and the shore
Presses it back upon its usual day.
Painted kites fly in the windy morning,
The ceaseless bustle and the ceaseless noise,
The clanking trams, the cries of rickshaw boys
Grow faint. But long before
The black and khaki ship is under way
The aggressive bugles bray
Announcing "Tiffin," while the passengers
Obedient and docile
Regardless of where he or she prefers
To sit, politely file
Like gentle horses entering their stables
To their appointed places at the tables.

Lines of chairs on the promenade deck,
Smell of engine room rising through hatches,
Mrs. Blake, with a sunburnt neck,
Organizing Shuffleboard matches,
Missionaries with pale, kind eyes,
Drained of colour by savage skies,
Strumming militantly glum
Hymns on a harmonium.

[17]

Flying fish from the bow waves skittering,
Mrs. Frobisher's endless tittering
And at night the great stars glittering.

Bugles blowing, deafening, insistent,
The Governor's Lady amiable but distant,
Returning home for six month's leave
A necessary, all too brief reprieve
From State Receptions, Women's Federations,
Official visits to remote plantations,
From garden parties under alien trees
And mocking, inefficient A.D.C.s.
Again the bugle's unrelenting blast,
Brown-sailed junks and sampans sailing past,
Clanging of ship's bells signalling the Watches,
Poor Mrs. Vining's unbecoming blotches;
All her own fault, when all is said and done,
For sleeping on the boat-deck in the sun.
Mrs. Ashpole, tremulously eager,
To pour out the minutia of her meagre
Unreflective, imperceptive mind.
Major Morpeth, coarse and unrefined,
Mrs. Morpeth, timid and retiring,
Both her daughters earnestly perspiring.
Colonel Wintringham, supreme at sports,
Tremendous knees beneath tremendous shorts,
Tremendous hands, tremendous calves and thighs
And small, submissive, vulnerable eyes.
Soup and water-biscuits at eleven,
Scampering of children over seven,
A fenced-in pen for children under five,
A frail old woman more dead than alive
Uninterested, withdrawn from social dramas,
Patiently tended by two Chinese Amahs.

Flying fish from the bow waves skittering,
Mrs. Frobisher's endless tittering
And at night the great stars glittering.

In Hong Kong, Mrs. Ashpole
Had an alarming experience
Which, without reticence,
After the ship had sailed again
She recounted in the saloon.
It appeared that she had lunched
At the Peninsular Hotel
(Which she knew well)
In Kowloon
And that later,
Crossing the harbour in the ferry
An American in a tussore suit said a very
Unpleasant word.
At first she imagined that she hadn't heard
Correctly
And said politely, circumspectly
"I beg your pardon"
Where upon he lewdly winked his eye
And, believe it or not,
Actually pinched her thigh!
Apparently she practically fainted
And if the ferry hadn't happened to reach the landing
At that very moment
She didn't know what she'd have done.
At all events she left him standing
And went off at a run
Feeling humiliated
And, you know, sort of tainted!
Fortunately she remembered
That she kept handy

In her bag
A tiny flask of brandy
From which she felt compelled to take a nip
In the rickshaw on the way back to the ship.

The ship arrived at dawn in Singapore
But in the city day had long begun
The wider streets were bland and empty still
But shops, beneath the flaking green arcades,
Blazed the shrill colours of their merchandise.
Dark rain clouds, harassed by the quickening light
Moved off across the flat metallic sea
And crouched upon the far horizon's edge
Like trained but savage circus animals
Awaiting sullenly their next performance.
Colonel Wintringham, in spotless drill,
Snuffing the air like an escaping prisoner,
Stepped firmly from the gangway to the dock
And strode, epitome of just authority,
Through raucous crowds of hotel porters, priests,
Beggars, vendors of bright, unlikely fruits,
Sellers of silks and cottons, ornaments,
Tortoise-shell and oriental beads
And, hailing a rickshaw boy in brisk Malay,
Settled himself at ease and bowled away.

Superficially like the sailor
With a wife in every port
Colonel Wintringham could depend
On finding an understanding friend
From Cape Town to Venezuela
Of a rather special sort.
The ship didn't sail till seven
And desire, like a rising stream,
Flooded Colonel Wintringham's kind,

Unregenerate, private mind.
And Oh for the secret heaven!
And Oh for the secret dream!

The siren hoots three times its final warning
The first one long, the second two much shorter,
Passengers at the deck-rail wave to friends
New life begins before the old life ends.
The lights reflected in the harbour water
Like yellow serpents twist
And Colonel Wintringham stands
As spick and span as, in the far off morning,
He'd set forth with his demons clamouring
His body tense, his pulses hammering,
To his peculiar tryst.
Now, only the faintest tremor of his hands
Betrays his recent, ardent sarabands.
Whistles are blown, the bugles shrilly bray again
The harbour sounds fade in the freshening breeze,
The crowded dock begins to slide away again.
Impassively the Colonel hears and sees
The last "Good-byes," the coloured streamers fluttering
And two pale nuns interminably muttering.

Mrs. Macomber in her steamer chair
Closed her tired eyes against the burning sky
And looked back over eighty-seven years
To when she was a child in Winchelsea.
The house was long and low, or so it seemed,
There was a sunken garden with small paths
Winding among bright flower beds, and beyond
The lichened red brick wall, an old, old tree
Stretched out its branches to the distant sea.
An orchard lay behind the house and Spring
Scattered its shaded grass with primroses

Later the catkins and the bluebells came
And there was a wooden swing.
Then memories of different years and different flowers
In different gardens flowed into her mind . . .

Five planter's children played Hide and Seek
Ran shrieking back and forth along the deck
White-coated stewards swooped between the chairs
Delivering bowls of soup and sandwiches.

But Mrs. Macomber stayed behind her eyes
Removed from all disturbance, quiet and still
Remembering other voyages long ago,
Remembering the walled city of Pekin
When first she went to live there as a bride;
The lacquered temples on the Western hills,
The early morning rides; watching the dawn
Staining with light the terra cotta plains;
The Empress Dowager, sharp and malign,
Monstrously attired in Highland tartan
Receiving Ministers at four A.M.,
And Mac, beloved Mac, in full court dress
Cursing Imperial capriciousness.
And then the children growing up and leaving
To cross these same warm seas to go to school;
The loving, dying, marrying and grieving,
The happy moments and the empty hours
Waiting for the news from England, waiting alone
In that blank echoing house in Wei Hai Wei.
Then suddenly, quite suddenly, when Mac was killed,
Becoming aware that youth and middle age
Had slipped into the past and were no more
And that there was little to look forward to
Beyond the changing seasons and the cold,
Niggardly compensations of the old.
Mrs. Macomber in her steamer chair

Closing her eyes against the burning sky
Knew, without terror and without despair,
That the time had come for her to die.

Mrs. Macomber was laid to rest at four forty-five P.M.
The ship reduced its speed and slowly, slowly came to a halt.
The missionaries provided a suitable Requiem
And a little grey cat ran out of a hatch which wasn't anyone's
    fault.
The Captain read the service which was mercifully brief.
The coffin slid into the water from under its covering flag
And one of the Chinese Amahs, assaulted by sudden grief,
Fumbled to find a handkerchief in a little beaded bag.
Mrs. Frobisher summed it all up that afternoon at tea
"There's nothing more impressive," she said, "than a burial at
    sea."

The ship pursues its course, the days go by
Romances bloom, tensions intensify.
Mrs. Macgrath and Mrs. Drage have words
Cawing and spluttering like angry birds
Until Mrs. Drage, with mottled, scarlet neck
Utters a strangled cry and leaves the deck.
That dreadful girl in the revealing jumper
Who had to be sent home from Kuala Lumpur
Is found, inside a lifeboat after dinner
Recumbent in the arms of Major Skinner.
Amusements are relentlessly devised
A Deck Quoits tournament is organized,
Competitors are bidden to confab in
The sacred precincts of the Captain's cabin.
A dance is given, fancy dress *de rigueur*
And Colonel Wintringham, his massive figure
Draped in a towel of enormous size
Coyly accepts the consolation prize.
The Deck Quoits tournament is fought and won

By Mr. Frith and Mrs. Cuthbertson.
The ship pursues its course, nights follow days,
The five piece orchestra tirelessly plays
Selections from the classics, German lieder,
Les Cloches de Corneville, Celeste Aida
And, as a musical salute to Asia,
Extracts from *The Mikado* and *The Geisha*.

Colombo, viewed from the approaching ship
Looked, in the distance, like bright coloured stones
Flung onto emerald and cinnabar hills
Behind which, serried ranks of mountains stood
Some of them veiled in cloud and some quite clear
Sharply defined against the morning sky.
Mrs. Frobisher, wearing shaded tones
Of pink and lavender, adorned with frills,
Emitting girlishly her usual trills
Of unprovoked amusement, stepped ashore
Escorted by the victorious Mr. Frith
Who'd given Mrs. Cuthbertson the slip
And, needing someone to go shopping with,
Had offered his services as cavalier.
Mrs. Frobisher knew Colombo well
And, prior to lunch at the Galle Face Hotel,
Led him immediately to a store
Where a be-turbaned, dark eyed Bengalese
Welcomed them with soft, obsequious sighs
And emptied from little chamois leather sacks
A scintillating, miscellaneous flood
Of zircons, amethysts, aquamarines,
Star sapphires, rubies pale as watered blood,
Opals, agates, cat's eyes, tourmalines
And cultured pearls as big as garden peas.
Poor Mr. Frith stared glumly at the stacks
Of gems, so few of which he could afford,
And wished to God that he'd remained on board.

However, after arguing awhile,
Appraising each small stone from every angle,
The Bengalese, to Mr. Frith's surprise,
Smiled with a patient, understanding smile
And finally agreed to compromise.
A set of tourmalines for Mrs. Frith
(Later to be set into a bangle)
Eight zircons, carefully matched, later to be
Fashioned with cunning ingenuity
Into some studs and links for evening dress,
Not flashy, mind you, but discreetly sober.
Then Mr. Frith, dazed by his own largesse,
Gave Mrs. Frobisher an opal pin
(Quite safe because her birth month was October).
The whole lot, plus a garnet crucifix
The Bengalese obligingly threw in,
Cost twenty-seven pounds, thirteen and six.

The Governor's Lady's steamer chair
Is set a little apart
And day after day she sits in it
And reads in it and knits in it
With a chiffon scarf to protect her hair
And loneliness in her heart.

She is sick of tropical greenery
And everything Asiatic
She is tired of lizards and parakeets,
Scarlet hibiscus and tom-tom beats
And her eyes are aching for scenery
That's a little bit less dramatic.

She seems immune from despairs and joys
Her bones are brittle with breeding.
It isn't easy to reconcile
Her unexpected, disarming smile
With the hard facade of her social poise
Which is definitely misleading.

She answers politely when addressed
Her coat has a Redfern label.
Inwardly timorous and shy
She goes through life with her head held high
And, indestructibly self-possessed,
Dines at the Captain's table.

The voyage continues, still the bugles blow,
Meal follows meal, the temperature below
Rises to quite unprecedented heights
Curbing the most voracious appetites.
Mrs. Drage, as though felled by a truncheon
Faints at the Purser's table during luncheon.
Outside, the Indian Ocean, stretched like glass,
Beneath a carapace of burnished brass,
Heaves with a gentle, oily under-swell
And Mrs. Vining, feeling far from well,
Suddenly gives a cry, clutches her head,
And runs precipitately to her bed.
But every evening, cold or hot,
Whether the sea is rough or not
Mr. Burden, Mr. Kapp
(The one that wears the yachting cap),
Mr. Haggerty from Rangoon,
Travelling with Mr. Witherspoon,
Bobby Green and "Nutty" Boyle
(Agents, both, from Standard Oil)
Mr. Randall, Harry Mott,
And tiny Mr. Appendrodt
Come rain, come shine, come joy, come doom,
Assemble in the smoking room.

These little men who travel far
How infinitely dull they are.
You find them in the ships that ply
Between Manila and Shanghai,

[26]

From Tripoli to Port Sudan,
Shimonosaki to Fusan.
You find them everywhere you go
And always in a P. and O.
These little men who travel far
Drinking forlornly at the bar
"This is my round" and then "One more"
"Stop me if you've heard this before"
Each one endeavouring to cap
The story of the other chap.
From Trinidad to Panama,
From Brindisi to Zanzibar,
From Alexandria to Crete,
These lethal *raconteurs* compete.
The loudest laugh, the coarsest joke,
Each shouting down the last who spoke,
Each ego straining more and more
Insensately to hold the floor.
The barman, with unsmiling eyes,
Smiles at such dismal vanities.
The smallest fish beneath the keel
With every fishy instinct feel
Each ancient pornographic quip
Stately descending through the ship
Until at last with one accord
They sink away, profoundly bored.
The little men who travel far
How sadly insecure they are.

A word must be said for Mrs. Rhys-Cunningham
Who embarked on the ship at Bombay
Accompanied by the Viscount Harringford,
The Honourable Evan and Mrs. Blair
And a little bird-like man called Ossie Blenkinsop
Who was the life and soul of the party
And made comments on everybody and everything

In a high-pitched, rather affected voice.
They had all been staying with some Maharajah
And Mrs. Rhys-Cunningham and Mrs. Blair
Appeared each night at dinner in different saris
Gossamer light, magenta, yellow and blue,
Threaded with gold and silver. Even the men
Wore tokens of their host's munificence;
Ossie had links like golden lotuses,
Blair and Lord Harringford, square signet rings
Of intricately carved chalcedony.
In the saloon they graced a separate table
Around which stewards hovered, thick as bees,
Tensed to anticipate their slightest wishes
Eagerly plying them with special dishes.

Lord Harringford had lustreless, blond hair
Smoothed back from a benign but narrow forehead
And, though his complexion was a trifle florid,
He had a certain charm, also of course
One felt he looked much better on a horse.
Unlike the Honourable Evan Blair
Who seemed, by Nature, wrought for an arm-chair.
Mrs. Blair was definitely jolly,
Thick-set and freckled with a raucous laugh,
One saw her tramping Dartmoor with a collie
Or, in some stately hall festooned with holly,
Handing out Christmas presents to the staff.

Mrs. Rhys-Cunningham's widowed state
Made little appeal for pity
Her taste in clothes was immaculate,
Her income, more than adequate
And her face extremely pretty.

Of weariness she showed no trace
In spite of her Indian Odysseys
Her figure was slim and she moved with grace
Along the deck's restricted space
Like one of the minor Goddesses.

She and her party remained aloof
Preoccupied and serene
From the *va et vient* and the warp and woof,
The daily recurring *Opéra Bouffe*
Of shipboard's defined routine.

So sure they were, so secure they were
So ineffably centrifugal
So set apart from the common weal,
Never in time for any meal
Disdainful of gong or bugle.

They failed to observe the looks of hate
The lips so cynically curved,
Tantalisingly intimate
They giggled and talked and stayed up late
Enclosed in their private world.

Between Bombay and the Gulf of Aden
An unexpected storm pounced in the night
And, seizing the ship like a ratting terrier,
Shook it and savaged it. The tranquil sea
As though bored by its own monotony
Rose up and, whipped by the shrieking wind,
Changed into ambulant, grey mountain peaks
Advancing endlessly, and in between
Their walls of grim implacability
Fell sickening valleys streaked with veins of foam.
The ship, reducing speed, received the first
Violent assault with shuddering acquiescence,
Pitching and tossing, rolling drunkenly,

Battered and bruised, sodden with flying spray,
She stubbornly proceeded on her way.
The cabins creaked and groaned: vases of flowers
Flew through the air as though endowed with wings,
Avalanches of books and toilet things
Tumbled onto the sleepers in their bunks
While, in the baggage room, enormous trunks
Rumbled and crashed with each vibrating roll.
Mrs. Macgrath, who'd left her porthole open,
Woke with a scream to see her lamé dress
Swirling about like some strange jellyfish
Together with her stockings, shoes and stays.
Poor Mr. Frith sustained a nasty graze
When the large plate of fruit he always kept
Handy beside his bunk, suddenly leapt
And struck him on the temple while he slept.
Colonel Wintringham, in a sarong
Which gave due freedom to his massive legs
And left his body bare, awoke to find
A broken bottle of green brilliantine
Clotting the matted hair upon his chest
Where it malignantly had come to rest.
Mrs. Frobisher arose and dressed
Uttering little moans and staggering,
The cabin stifled her, it lurched and heaved
Flinging her to and fro like a rag doll.
When finally her object was achieved
She sank disconsolate on her bunk
Armed with a lifebelt and two winter coats,
And waited to be conducted to the boats.
Meanwhile the Governor's Lady, unafraid,
Asked the night stewardess to call her maid.
All the next day the hurricane continued,
Screamed through the rigging, tore at the plunging masts,
Hatches were battened down, the deck doors guarded
By weary stewards empowered to prevent

Foolhardy passengers with iron stomachs
From venturing out to photograph the sea.
In the saloon "fiddles" encased the tables,
Ropes were stretched taut across the creaking decks,
Stewards and stewardesses with covered basins
Swayed doggedly along the corridors
Moving unflurried through familiar hells
Of retchings, groanings and incessant bells.
In the deserted lounge, in time for tea,
The five piece orchestra, reduced to three,
Valiantly and to its undying glory
Obliged with *Tosca* and *Il Trovatore*.
In the late afternoon, capriciously,
The storm clouds parted on the starboard beam
Revealing a strip of blue, unflurried sky.

An hour later, in a blaze of sun
The ship still wallowed, but the storm was done.

The sun beats down on Aden. The port officials drip,
The dusty buildings sizzle in the heat,
The grimy, black coal barges crowd obscenely round the ship
Like gaping coffins on a metal sheet.
The town has few attractions: no shaded avenues,
No fascinating vistas to explore.
The passengers have only two alternatives to choose,
To suffocate on board or go ashore.
Those who decide the latter is the less repellent plan
From the point of view of culture, draw a blank,
For they find the arid town has little more to offer than
Two so-called mermaids in a dingy tank.
These strange, misshapen creatures, constricted and morose,
Hauled up long since in some bewildering net
Stare fishily, unseeingly, when visitors draw close,
Grateful at least, at least, for being wet.
Just before evening when the brazen sky begins to cool

The ship sails and the harbour fades from view
Astern, the wake, unwinding like white ribbon from a spool
Stretches and coils upon the deepening blue
And Aden, stumbling back against the night
Suddenly beautiful, sinks out of sight.

From either bank of the Suez Canal
The desert marches to the sky
And, on the interminable sand
Stretching away to the Promised Land
Lean, meditative Arabs stand
Watching the ship go by.
So narrow is the waterway
You feel that by stretching out an arm
You could touch the hovels of mud and clay
Or pick a date from a dusty palm.
On the other side, beyond the day,
Beyond the night, the Sahara spills,
Beyond immediate prophecy
So far as to challenge Infinity
Until it at last, at last gives way
To lakes and beginnings of hills,
And then the tropics where coloured birds
Swift in flight as a falling star
Swoop over lumbering elephant herds
And the fevered jungles of Africa.

At Port Said, Mr. Frith and Mrs. Frobisher
Who'd been inseparable since Colombo
Strolled in the evening through crowded streets,
Mrs. Frobisher dressed to the nines
Looking about her eagerly for signs
Indicative of strange exotic vices
For which the unattractive little town
Had, quite inaccurately, won renown.
They sat outside a café eating ices

Badgered by beggars and by fortune tellers
By urchins bearing trays of vivid sweets
By servile Oriental carpet-sellers
Whose voices fluctuated with their prices.
The "Gully-Gully" merchant's mumbo-jumbo
Left them depressed and dully mystified.
They watched, with lassitude, the agile tricks
Vanishing coins, recurrent baby chicks,
All the impressive, boring sleight of hand
Which nobody could ever understand.
Later they rose, jostled by "lesser breeds"
Deafened by mendicant, subservient whining
And saw Mrs. Macgrath and Mrs. Vining
Bargaining for synthetic amber beads.
Presently Colonel Wintringham went by
Striding with back erect and shoulders high
And, trotting purposefully by his side,
A picturesque but dubious Arab guide.
Mrs. Rhys-Cunningham wandered through the crowd
Accompanied by Ossie and the Blairs
Who, when Mrs. Frobisher politely bowed,
Acknowledged her with vaguely puzzled stares.
A seedy man drew Mr. Frith apart
And swiftly flashed before his startled gaze
A snapshot of an ageing Syrian tart
Placidly naked, fastening her stays.
Later they tried to dissipate their gloom
With champagne cocktails in the smoking room.

    The Mediterranean welcomed the ship
    And flattered her with promises
    Of cleaner airs and fresher winds
    And Europe drawing slowly closer.
    Deck games were played with keener zest
    And here and there fur coats appeared
    And one dark night on the starboard side

Stromboli, spurting flame, defied
The gentle sea and the quiet sky.
Later the mountains of Sicily
Painted lavender shadows against
A blazing sunset of green and rose.
The Shuffleboard finals came and went
With Mrs. Blake the ultimate winner.
The second prize went to Major Skinner
And the Captain gave a gala dinner.
After Marseilles the atmosphere on board
Altered perceptibly. In the saloon
Passengers, by mutual accord,
Tacitly moved from their allotted places,
Closed up the ranks, filled in the gaps, ignored
The hitherto stern protocol, and soon
Banished from memory the familiar faces
Of those who had so treacherously planned
To leave the ship and go home overland.
Europe slid by upon the starboard side
To port, Africa hid below the sea
Gibraltar rose impressive, dignified
Knowing no rising sun could ever set
On such a symbol of Imperial pride
On such invulnerable majesty.
That night, the Rock, an ebon silhouette
Through Colonel Wintringham's binoculars
Vanished at last among the swaying stars.

The Bay of Biscay, true to form
Behaved in its usual way
Greeting the ship with rain and storm
And gunmetal seas and spray.
Once more the cabins creaked and groaned
Once more the wind through the rigging moaned
Like sinners on Judgement Day.
The gale blew stronger and lashed the waves

Like an overseer with a whip
The rain blew level as music staves
From bow to stern of the ship.
Poor Mrs. Vining, the sport of fate
Fell, embedding her upper plate
In the flesh of her lower lip.
But when the tempest had ceased to roar
And had muted its sullen arrogance
And the stubborn vessel at last forbore
To bow to the ocean's exigence
The clouds dispersed, the horizon cleared
Some pale, unconvincing stars appeared
And Mrs. Cuthbertson swore she saw
A light on the coast of France.

Of course there was a ship's concert
There is always a ship's concert
Given ostensibly in aid of the Seamen's Fund
Given ostensibly to divert the passengers
But really given for several other reasons.
The Seamen's Fund, we know, accrues some benefit
The passengers, we know, are fairly diverted
But over and above and behind and below
These clear, unquestionable advantages
There are other issues, other implications.
The battle of straining egos for the light
For that sweet hour of temporary recognition,
There is also to be considered the Purser's pride
The raging hunger in him to be satisfied
Once, once at least in course of every voyage.
How can he carry on each day's routine
Pacify passengers, deal with small complaints
Keep a sharp, suave and understanding eye
On diverse temperaments, without some hope
Of one rich moment when subservience ends
And he at least can dominate awhile

Those, who by wealth and rank and circumstance
Are classified as his superiors?
At the ship's concert he can rise
Clad in benign authority and speak
A few well chosen introductory phrases.
Later, like other Deities, rise again
And make a longer, more imposing speech,
Thanking the artists, thanking the orchestra
Thanking the Captain for his gracious presence
Thanking the audience for their kind reception
Thanking the universe, the moon and stars
For this dear, golden opportunity
To stand, upholder of a worthy cause
And hear the sound of personal applause.
The concert started with *Veronique*
Played excessively loudly
And when it came to "Swing High, Swing Low"
Mrs. Blake, in the second row,
Hummed the melody proudly.
Then a young man of strong physique
With the air of a swaggering rebel
Embarked to everyone's surprise
On "Take a Pair of Sparkling Eyes"
In a voice that was almost treble.
Next came a girl from the Second Class
With spectacles and a fiddle
Who, unaware that she was tone deaf
Played Rubinstein's "Melody in F"
And lost her place in the middle.
A table steward with lungs of brass
Bellowed a song of Devon
And Colonel Wintringham, drenched in sweat,
With Mrs. Drage, sang an arch duet
Entitled "The Keys of Heaven."
A boy in a Javanese sarong
Made everyone rather restive

By executing a native dance
Which, whether on purpose or by chance,
Was definitely suggestive.
Turn followed turn, song followed song
Until all at last was ended
And the Purser's ears, crimson with praise,
Re-echoed the Governor's Lady's phrase
"It has all been simply splendid!"

England at last. At first only a smudge
A blue smudge on a windy blue-grey morning
High mackerel sky and spray, barely discernible
Splintering white against the sullen rocks,
The granite obstinacy of Land's End.
Seagulls appear, one perches in the rigging,
Its curved beak like a yellow scimitar.
Passengers crowd the rails, eager to catch
The first glimpse, after months and years away
Of their beloved and inalienable home.
This is a moment that must be remembered
Set in the heart and mind, branded upon
The retinas of tired English eyes,
Tired of violent colours, tired of glare
And heat and sand and jungles and bright birds.
Eyes that so often longingly have gazed
Through beaded curtains of torrential rain
To gentler rain falling on English woods,
Eyes that have stared nostalgically beyond
Flowers too vivid in the blazing light
To quieter flowers in herbaceous borders
Snapdragons, Pinks, Sweet Williams, Lupins, Phlox
And gawky, unexotic Hollyhocks.
The ship draws nearer to the welcoming land
Houses are visible, cottages white and grey
Scramble down between low, forbidding cliffs
To crescent coves of shining golden sand

And twisted harbours filled with fishing boats.
The Lizard, crouching among its little waves
Inspires Mrs. Vining to recall
That, when she was a girl of seventeen
Together with two cousins and a friend
She got caught by the tide at Kynance Cove
And had to spend several hours upon a ledge
Wet and bedraggled, frightened and woebegone
Until the coastguards came and rescued them.
The ship, most courteously, draws nearer still
And steams along less than a mile from shore.
Falmouth, Veryan, Porthpean, St. Austell Bay
Fowey, Looe, Polperro, all identified
By Mrs. Vining's overwhelming pride
At being the only one on board who "Knew
Her Cornwall inside out and through and through."

The Eddystone Lighthouse, slim and white
Like a pencil stuck in the blue,
Plymouth Hoe and Babbacombe Bay
Gaunt rocks changing from red to grey
Until the slow diminishing light
Banishes them from view.

No one on board can quite relax
Poor Mr. Frith gets drunk
And Mrs. Frobisher, bathed in tears,
Sits, surrounded by souvenirs
Each one of which she carefully packs
With her hopes, in her cabin trunk.

Colonel Wintringham cannot sleep
Barred are the gates of Slumberland
He cannot make up his mind between
His sister's cottage at Bushey Green
A trip to the Continent on the cheap
Or a walking tour in Northumberland.

Inscrutable, disconsolate
Remote from understanding
Counting the dark hours as they pass
Wide awake in the Second Class
Mrs. Macomber's Amahs wait
To be told where to go on landing.

How evil the mind's continued rage!
How cruel the heart that hardens!
Aware of this truth, with smiling face
And overflowering with Christian grace,
Mrs. Macgrath asks Mrs. Drage
To tea in Ennismore Gardens.

Last minute packing finished and done
The long and wearisome journey over
The Governor's Lady, standing apart,
With a sudden lifting of her heart
Sees, like sentinels in the sun,
The arrogant cliffs of Dover.

Kent on the one side, Essex on the other
And the wide Thames Estuary lying in between.
Oilers, Tankers, Cargo-ships and Tug-boats,
The churning yellow paddles of *The Margate Queen.*
Cockneys on a holiday, sound of concertinas
Vying with the seagulls squawking in the breeze,
Houses, wharves and factories, grey beside the river,
Behind them, marshes and a few tall trees.
Delicately, shrewdly, the black-funnelled liner
Dark hull whitened by the salt sea spray
Picks her way with dignity among her lesser sisters
And steams up to Tilbury through the warm June day.

This then is the end. The end of longing,
The realised anticipatory dream,
The lovely moment, still unspoiled and tremulous

Still lighter than a bubble, gay with hope,
Still free from anti-climax, before Time
Itself has had the time to tarnish it.
The image of homecoming still unmarred
By little disappointments, small delays
And sudden, inexplicable dismays.

The siren hoots three times, three warning calls,
The first one long, the second two much shorter.
And into the turgid, swirling river water
The anchor falls.

BORA BORA

The wide lagoon in which the island lies
Changes its colours with the changing skies
And, lovely beyond belief,
The dazzling surf upon the outer reef
Murmurs its lonely, timeless lullaby
Warning the heart perhaps that life is brief
Measured against the sea's eternity.

In the lagoon beneath the surface grow
Wild fantasies of coral; to and fro
And, lovely beyond all praise,
The vivid fish interminably graze:
Rubies and emeralds, yellows, blues and mauves
Endlessly nibbling at the coral sprays
Endlessly flitting through the coral groves.

The coco-palms paint shadows on the sand
Shadows that dance a languid saraband
And, lovely indeed to see,
Above the scented frangipani tree
The mountain's silhouette against the moon
Who, as she saunters through Infinity
Traces a silver path on the lagoon.

VENICE

Last Wednesday on the Piazza
Near San Marco's trecento Duomo
I observed una grassa ragazza
With a thin, Middle Western uomo.

He was swatting a piccolo mosca
She was eating a chocolate gelato
While an orchestra played (from *La Tosca*)
A flat violin obbligato.

They stared at a dusty piccione
They spoke not a single parola
She ordered some Te con limone
He ordered an iced Coca-Cola.

And while the tramanto del sole
Set fire to the Grande Canale
She scribbled haphazard parole
On glazed Cartoline Postale.

NOTHING IS LOST

Deep in our subconscious, we are told
Lie all our memories, lie all the notes
Of all the music we have ever heard
And all the phrases those we loved have spoken,
Sorrows and losses time has since consoled,
Family jokes, out-moded anecdotes
Each sentimental souvenir and token
Everything seen, experienced, each word
Addressed to us in infancy, before
Before we could even know or understand
The implications of our wonderland.
There they all are, the legendary lies
The birthday treats, the sights, the sounds, the tears
Forgotten debris of forgotten years
Waiting to be recalled, waiting to rise
Before our world dissolves before our eyes
Waiting for some small, intimate reminder,
A word, a tune, a known familiar scent
An echo from the past when, innocent
We looked upon the present with delight
And doubted not the future would be kinder
And never knew the loneliness of night.

EPITAPH FOR AN ELDERLY ACTRESS

She got in a rage
About age
And retired, in a huff, from the stage.
Which, taken all round, was a pity
Because she was still fairly pretty
But she got in a rage
About age.

She burst into tears
It appears
When the rude, inconsiderate years
Undermined her once flawless complexion
And whenever she saw her reflection
In a mirror, she burst into tears
It appears.

She got in a state
About weight
And resented each morsel she ate.
Her colon she constantly sluiced
And reduced and reduced and reduced
And, at quite an incredible rate
Put on weight.

She got in a rage
About age
But she still could have played "Mistress Page"

And she certainly could have done worse
Than "Hay Fever" or "Juliet's Nurse"
But she got in a terrible rage
About age.

And she moaned and she wept and she wailed
And she roared and she ranted and railed
And retired, very heavily veiled,
From the stage.

ANY PART OF PIGGY

Any part of piggy
Is quite all right with me
Ham from Westphalia, ham from Parma
Ham as lean as the Dalai Lama
Ham from Virginia, ham from York,
Trotters, sausages, hot roast pork.
Crackling crisp for my teeth to grind on
Bacon with or without the rind on
Though humanitarian
I'm not a vegetarian.
I'm neither crank nor prude nor prig
And though it may sound infra dig
Any part of darling pig
Is perfectly fine with me.

I'M HERE FOR A SHORT VISIT ONLY

I'm here for a short visit only
And I'd rather be loved than hated
Eternity may be lonely
When my body's disintegrated
And that which is loosely termed my soul
Goes whizzing off through the infinite
By means of some vague, remote control
I'd like to think I was missed a bit.

I AM NO GOOD AT LOVE

I am no good at love
My heart should be wise and free
I kill the unfortunate golden goose
Whoever it may be
With over-articulate tenderness
And too much intensity.

I am no good at love
I batter it out of shape
Suspicion tears at my sleepless mind
And, gibbering like an ape,
I lie alone in the endless dark
Knowing there's no escape.

I am no good at love
When my easy heart I yield
Wild words come tumbling from my mouth
Which should have stayed concealed
And my jealousy turns a bed of bliss
Into a battlefield.

I am no good at love
I betray it with little sins
For I feel the misery of the end
In the moment that it begins
And the bitterness of the last good-bye
Is the bitterness that wins.

TO L. R-M.

There are certain ladies in our land,
Still living and still unafraid
Whose hearts have known a lot of pain,
Whose eyes have shed so many tears,
Who welcome pity with disdain
And view the fast encroaching years
Humorously and undismayed.

There are certain ladies in our land,
Whose courage is too deeply bred
To merit unreflecting praise.
For them no easy, glib escape;
No mystic hopes confuse their days
They can identify the shape
Of what's to come, devoid of dread.

There are certain ladies in our land
Who bring to Life the gift of gay
Uncompromising sanity.
The past, for them, is safe and sure.
Perhaps their only vanity
Is that they know they can endure
The rigours of another day.

REUNION

"It's lovely to have you back" she said
  But the tone was pitched too high
He, sitting opposite, crumbled a roll
Made like a crescent with black seeds on it,
Lit a cigarette and tried to smile;
A gesture devastating in its hopelessness,
A gallant effort, gallantly designed
To reassure her, an abortive, brave attempt
To cut at least a temporary clearing
In the surrounding jungle. She smiled back
Seeing him, for an instant, suddenly
Clearly and vividly as he once had been
Before the cruel, separating years
Had altered everything. She turned away
And fumbled in her bag to hide her tears.
Outside the open window, light summer rain
Had left a sheen on the Soho street
Reflecting stars and moon and Neon lights
At the feet of strange characters
Shuffling back and forth, pausing at corners
To whisper in alien tongues and then retire
Back into the shadows.
Inside the restaurant the customers sat
Encased in impersonal, synthetic cosiness
There were small red lamps on all the tables
And rather untidy vases of anemones,

Whenever the service door swung open
There was a smell of garlic and frying fat
And the noise of banging crockery in the kitchen.

When the Maître d'Hôtel brought the menu
The atmosphere eased a little
Because there was something to say.
He was sallow and swarthy, the Maître d'Hôtel
With sadness in his chocolate coloured eyes,
Suddenly she longed to catch at his coat tails and cry
(In Italian of course) "Cheer up—cheer up.
You'll be going home some day
Home to your own place, your own familiar unhygienic village
With the olive groves rolling up to the sky
And the Campanile and the Piazza
Where the people you really know pass by"
But he took their order and went away
And at their table the silence lay
And the evening stretched before them
Bleak, desolate and grey
With so much so much so much to think
And so little, so little to say.

CONDOLENCE

The mind, an inveterate traveller
Journeys swiftly and far
Faster than light, quicker than sound
Or the flaming arc of a falling star
But the body remains in a vacuum
Gagged, bound and sick with dread
Knowing the words that can't be spoken
Searching for words that must be said
Dumb, inarticulate, heartbroken.
Inadequate, inhibited.

A QUESTION OF VALUES

Christopher Marlowe or Francis Bacon
    The author of "Lear" remains unshaken
Willie Herbert or Mary Fitton
    What does it matter? The Sonnets were written.

TRIBUTE TO MARLENE DIETRICH

We know God made trees
And the birds and the bees
And seas for the fishes to swim in
We are also aware
That he has quite a flair
For creating exceptional women.
Where Eve said to Adam
"Start calling me Madam"
The world became far more exciting
Which turns to confusion
The modern delusion
That sex is a question of lighting.
For female allure
Whether pure or impure
Has seldom reported a failure
As I know and you know
From Venus and Juno
Right down to *La Dame aux Camélias*.
This glamour, it seems,
Is the substance of dreams
To the most imperceptive perceiver
The Serpent of Nile
Could achieve with a smile
Far quicker results than Geneva.
Though we all might enjoy
Seeing Helen of Troy

As a gay, cabaret entertainer
I doubt that she could
Be one quarter as good
As our legendary, lovely Marlene.

SOCIAL GRACE

I expect you've heard this a million times before
But I absolutely adored your last play
I went four times—and now to think
That here I am actually talking to you!
It's thrilling! Honestly it is, I mean,
It's always thrilling isn't it to meet someone really celebrated?
I mean someone who really does things.
I expect all this is a terrible bore for you.
After all you go everywhere and know everybody.
It must be wonderful to go absolutely everywhere
And know absolutely everybody and—Oh dear—
Then to have to listen to someone like me,
I mean someone absolutely ordinary just one of your public.
No one will believe me when I tell them
That I have actually been talking to the great man himself.
It must be wonderful to be so frightfully brainy
And know all the things that you know.
I'm not brainy a bit, neither is my husband,
Just plain humdrum that's what we are.
But we do come up to town occasionally
And go to shows and things. Actually my husband
Is quite a good critic, not professionally of course,
What I mean is that he isn't all that easily pleased.
He doesn't like everything. Oh no not by any means.
He simply hated that thing at the Haymarket
Which everybody went on about. "Rubbish," he said,
Straight out like that, "Damned Rubbish!"

I nearly died because heaps of people were listening.
But that's quite typical of him. He just says what he thinks.
And he can't stand all this highbrow stuff—
Do you know what I mean?—All these plays about people being
    miserable
And never getting what they want and not even committing suicide
But just being absolutely wretched. He says he goes to the theatre
To have a good time. That's why he simply loves all your things,
I mean they relax him and he doesn't have to think.
And he certainly does love a good laugh.
You should have seen him the other night when we went to that film
With what's-her-name in it—I can't remember the title.
I thought he'd have a fit, honestly I did.
You must know the one I mean, the one about the man who comes
    home
And finds his wife has been carrying on with his best friend
And of course he's furious at first and then he decides to teach her a
    lesson.
You must have seen it. I wish I could remember the name
But that's absolutely typical of me, I've got a head like a sieve,
I keep on forgetting things and as for names—well!
I just cannot for the life of me remember them.
Faces yes, I never forget a face because I happen to be naturally
    observant
And always have been ever since I was a tiny kiddie
But names! Oh dear! I'm quite hopeless.
I feel such a fool sometimes
I do honestly.

PERSONAL REMINISCENCE

I cannot remember
I cannot remember
The house where I was born
But I know it was in Waldegrave Road
Teddington, Middlesex
Not far from the border of Surrey
An unpretentious abode
Which, I believe,
Economy forced us to leave
In rather a hurry.
But I *can* remember my grandmother's Indian shawl
Which, although exotic to behold,
Felt cold.
Then there was a framed photograph in the hall
Of my father wearing a Norfolk jacket,
Holding a bicycle and tennis racquet
And leaning against a wall
Looking tenacious and distinctly grim
As though he feared they'd be whisked away from him.
I can also remember with repulsive clarity
Appearing at a concert in aid of charity
At which I sang, not the "Green Hill Far Away" that you know
But the one by Gounod.
I remember a paperweight made of quartz
And a sombre Gustave Doré engraving
Illustrating the Book of Revelations
Which, I am told, upset my vibrations.

I remember too a most peculiar craving
For "Liquorice All-Sorts"
Then there was a song, "Oh that we two were Maying"
And my uncle, who later took to the bottle, playing
And playing very well
An organ called the "Mustel"
I remember the smell of rotting leaves
In the Autumn quietness of suburban roads
And seeing the Winter river flooding
And swirling over the tow-path by the lock.
I remember my cousin Doris in a party frock
With Broderie Anglaise at the neck and sleeves
And being allowed to stir the Christmas pudding
On long ago, enchanted Christmas Eves,
All this took place in Teddington, Middlesex
Not far from the Surrey border
But none of these little episodes
None of the things I call to mind
None of the memories I find
Are in chronological order
Is in chronological order.

MRS MALLORY

Mrs. Mallory went to a Psychiatrist
On the advice of Mrs. Silvera
Who had been twice divorced
And considered herself to be maladjusted.
Mrs. Mallory, who had never been divorced at all,
Considered that she also was maladjusted
Not for any specific reason really
Nothing you could put your finger on
But a definite feeling of dissatisfaction
With life in general and Mr. Mallory in particular,
And Deidre too who was no comfort and solace to her mother
Though at her age she should have been
But she was an unpredictable character
Who devoted too much time to Rock-n-Roll
And none at all to domestic science
And helping in the house and keeping a wary eye open
For Mr. Right to come along and sweep her away
To a series of social triumphs
In Washington possibly, or at least Baltimore,
Which Mrs. Mallory could read about in the gossip columns
And then send the cuttings to Irma in Minneapolis
Who would have to read them whether she liked it or not.

Mrs. Mallory lay on the Psychiatrist's sofa
With her arms relaxed at her sides
And her feet sticking up, one to the right and one to the left
Like a mermaid's tail.

The Psychiatrist sat behind her out of range
And waited politely for her to begin to talk
Which she was only too eager to do
After the first shyness had worn off
And he had asked her a few routine questions.
But she talked and talked and talked and talked.
So much, so much came tumbling out of her,
More than she would ever have believed possible,
But then of course, unlike Mrs. Silvera, he didn't interrupt
And say things like, "That reminds me of when I went to Atlantic
    City
With my first husband" or "I feel exactly the same dear naturally
But I have to control my feelings on account of being so strictly
    raised."
The Psychiatrist didn't seem to be reminded of anything at all.
He sat there so quietly that once Mrs. Mallory looked round
To see if he had dropped off, but he hadn't;
There he was scribbling away on a pad and occasionally
        nodding his head.
She told him all about Deidre
And Mr. Mallory coming home from the Rotarian lunch
And taking his pants off on the landing
And shouting "Everything I have is yours, you're part of me!"
So loudly that Beulah had come out of the kitchen
And seen him with all his lower parts showing
And his hat still on.
She also told the Psychiatrist about the man in the subway
Who had pressed himself against her from behind
And said something that sounded like "Ug Ug"
Which was the one thing she had never told Mrs. Silvera
Perhaps on account of her having been so strictly raised.
She told him as well about the extraordinary dream she had had
On the night following the Beedmeyers' Anniversary party
But when she was in the middle of it,
Before she had even got to the bit about the horse,

[61]

He rose and smiled and said that he hoped to see her next
    Friday
At the same time.
So she got up from the couch
Feeling a little dizzy and aware that her left foot had gone to
    sleep
But when she stamped it it was all right.
She felt much better when she got home
And much less maladjusted
And when Mr. Mallory came home from the office
She had put on her new hostess gown
Which she had only worn twice
Once at the Beedmeyers and the other time at the Palisades
    Country Club
On Christmas Eve.
Also she had rubbed some Shalimar behind her ears
And greeted him with an all-embracing, welcoming smile
But it was none of it any use really
When dinner was over they looked at Television as they always
    did
Until it was time to go to bed,
Mr. Mallory spent longer in the bathroom than usual
And the Shalimar began to wear off.
But when he did come back in his pajamas
It didn't seem to matter much anyway
Because he merely belched and said "Excuse me" automatically,
Blew her a perfunctory kiss and got into his own bed,
Later on, after he had read *McCall's* for a little,
He switched off the light.

Mrs. Mallory lay in the darkness
With her arms relaxed at her sides
And her feet up, one to the right and one to the left
Like a mermaid's tail
And a tear rolled down her face all the way to her chin.

HONEYMOON (1905)

"They were married
And lived happily ever after."
But before living happily ever after
They drove to Paddington Station
Where, acutely embarrassed, harassed
And harried;
Bruised by excessive jubilation
And suffering from strain
They got into a train
And, having settled themselves in a reserved carriage,
Sought relief, with jokes and nervous laughter,
From the sudden, frightening awareness of their marriage.

Caught in the web their fate had spun
They watched the suburbs sliding by,
Rows of small houses, neatly matched,
Safe, respectable, semi-detached;
Lines of gardens like pale green stripes,
Men in shirtsleeves smoking pipes
Making the most of a watery sun
In a watery English sky.

Then pollarded willows and the river curving
Between high trees and under low grey bridges
Flowing through busy locks, looping and swerving
Past formal gardens bright with daffodils.
Further away the unpretentious hills

Rising in gentle, misty ridges,
Quiet, insular, and proud
Under their canopies of cloud.

Presently the silence between them broke,
Edward, tremulous in his new tweed suit
And Lavinia, pale beneath her violet toque,
Opened the picnic-basket, lovingly packed
By loving hands only this morning—No!
Those sardine sandwiches were neatly stacked
Lost centuries ago.
The pale, cold chicken, hard-boiled eggs and fruit
The cheese and biscuits and Madeira cake
Were all assembled in another life
Before "I now pronounce you man and wife"
Had torn two sleepers suddenly awake
From all that hitherto had been a dream
And cruelly hurled
Both of them, shivering, into this sweeping stream
This alien, mutual unfamiliar world.

A little later, fortified by champagne
They sat, relaxed but disinclined to talk
Feeling the changing rhythms of the train
Bearing them onward through West country towns
Outside in the half light, serene and still,
They saw the fading Somersetshire Downs
And, gleaming on the side of a smooth, long hill
A white horse carved in chalk.

Later still, in a flurry of rain
They arrived at their destination
And with panic gripping their hearts again
They drove from the noisy station
To a bright, impersonal double room
In the best hotel in Ilfracombe.

[64]

They opened the window and stared outside
At the outline of a curving bay,
At dark cliffs crouching in the spray
And wet sand bared by the falling tide.
The scudding clouds and the rain-furrowed sea
Mocked at their desperate chastity.
Inside the room the gas globes shed,
Contemptuous of their bridal night,
A hard, implacable yellow light
On a hard, implacable double bed.

The fluted mahogany looking glass
Reflected their prison of blazing brass,
Crude, unendurable, unkind.
And then, quite suddenly, with a blind
Instinctive gesture of loving grace,
She lifted her hand and touched his face.

THE BOY ACTOR

I can remember. I can remember.
The months of November and December
    Were filled for me with peculiar joys
So different from those of other boys
    For other boys would be counting the days
Until end of term and holiday times
    But I was acting in Christmas plays
While they were taken to pantomimes.
    I didn't envy their Eton suits,
Their children's dances and Christmas trees.
    My life had wonderful substitutes
For such conventional treats as these.
    I didn't envy their country larks,
Their organised games in panelled halls:
    While they made snow men in stately parks
I was counting the curtain calls.

        I remember the auditions, the nerve-racking auditions:
        Darkened auditorium and empty, dusty stage,
        Little girls in ballet dresses practising "positions"
        Gentlemen with pince-nez asking you your age.
        Hopefulness and nervousness struggling within you,
        Dreading that familiar phrase, "Thank you dear, no more."
        Straining every muscle, every tendon, every sinew
        To do your dance much better than you'd ever done
            before.

Think of your performance. Never mind the others,
Never mind the pianist, talent must prevail.
Never mind the baleful eyes of other children's mothers
Glaring from the corners and willing you to fail.

I can remember. I can remember.
The months of November and December
    Were more significant to me
Than other months could ever be
    For they were the months of high romance
When Destiny waited on tiptoe,
    When every boy actor stood a chance
Of getting into a Christmas show,
    Not for me the dubious heaven
Of being some prefect's protégé
    Not for me the Second Eleven.
For me, two performances a day.

    Ah those first rehearsals! Only very few lines:
    Rushing home to mother, learning them by heart,
    "Enter Left through window"—Dots to mark the cue
        lines:
    "Exit with the others"—Still it *was* a part.
    Opening performance; legs a bit unsteady,
    Dedicated tension, shivers down my spine,
    Powder, grease and eye-black, sticks of make-up ready
    Leichner number three and number five and number
        nine.
    World of strange enchantment, magic for a small boy
    Dreaming of the future, reaching for the crown,
    Rigid in the dressing room, listening for the call-boy
    "Overture Beginners—Everybody Down!"

I can remember. I can remember.
The months of November and December,
    Although climatically cold and damp,

Meant more to me than Aladdin's lamp.
I see myself, having got a job,
Walking on wings along the Strand,
Uncertain whether to laugh or sob
And clutching tightly my mother's hand,
    I never cared who scored the goal
Or which side won the silver cup,
    I never learned to bat or bowl
But I heard the curtain going up.

DO I BELIEVE

Do I believe in God?
Well yes, I suppose, in a sort of way.
It's really terribly hard to say.
I'm sure that there must be of course
Some kind of vital, motive force,
Some power that holds the winning cards
Behind life's ambiguous facades
But whether you think me odd or not
I can't decide if it's God or not.

I look at the changing sea and sky
And try to picture Eternity
I gaze at immensities of blue
And say to myself "It can't be true
That somewhere up in that abstract sphere
Are all the people who once were here
Attired in white and shapeless gowns
Sitting on clouds like eiderdowns
Plucking at harps and twanging lutes
With cherubim in their birthday suits,
Set in an ageless, timeless dream
Part of a formulated scheme
Formulated before the flood
Before the Amoeba left the mud
And, stranded upon a rocky shelf
Proceeded to subdivide itself."

I look at the changing sea and sky
And try to picture Infinity.
I gaze at a multitude of stars
Envisaging the men on Mars
Wondering if they too are torn
Between their sunset and their dawn
By dreadful, night-engendered fears
Of what may lie beyond their years
And if they too, through thick and thin,
Are dogged by consciousness of Sin.
Have they, to give them self-reliance,
A form of Martian Christian Science?
Or do they live in constant hope
Of dispensations from some Pope?

Are they pursued from womb to tomb
By hideous prophecies of doom?
Have they cathedral, church or chapel
Are they concerned with Adam's apple?
Have they immortal souls like us
Or are they less presumptuous?

Do I believe in God?
I can't say No and I can't say Yes
To me it's anybody's guess
But if all's true that we once were told
Before we grew wise and sad and old
When finally Death rolls up our eyes
We'll find we're in for a big surprise.

When Queen Victoria died
The whole of England mourned
Not for a so recently breathing old woman
A wife and a mother and a widow,
Not for a staunch upholder of Christendom,
A stickler for etiquette
A vigilant arbiter of moral values
But for a symbol.
A symbol of security and prosperity
Of "My Country Right or Wrong"
Of "Good is good and Bad is bad"
And "What was good enough for my father
Ought to be good enough for you"
And "If you don't eat your tapioca pudding
You will be locked in your bedroom
And given nothing but bread and water
Over and over again until you come to your senses"
And are weak and pale and famished and say
Breathlessly, hopelessly and with hate in your heart
"Please Papa I would now like some tapioca pudding very
        much indeed"
A symbol too of proper elegance
Not the flaunting, bejewelled kind
That later became so popular
But a truly proper elegance,
An elegance of the spirit,
Of withdrawal from unpleasant subjects

Such as Sex and Poverty and Pit Ponies
And Little Children working in the Mines
And Rude Words and Divorce and Socialism
And numberless other inadmissible horrors.
When Queen Victoria died
They brought her little body from the Isle of Wight
Closed up in a black coffin, finished and done for,
With no longer any feelings and regrets and Memories of
    Albert
And no more blood pumping through the feeble veins
And no more heart beating away
As it had beaten for so many tiring years.
The coffin was placed upon a gun-carriage
And drawn along sadly and slowly by English sailors.

But long before this the people had mourned
And walked about the streets and the Parks and Kensington
    Gardens
Silently, solemnly and dressed in black.
Now, with the news already a few days old
The immediate shock had faded.
The business of the funeral was less poignant than the first
    realisation of death,
This was a pageant, right and fitting, but adjustments were already
    beginning to be made.
This was something we were all used to,
This slow solemnity
This measured progress to the grave.
If it hadn't been for the gun-carriage
And the crowds and all the flags at half mast
And all the shops being closed
It might just as well have been Aunt Cordelia
Who died a few months earlier in Torquay
And had to be brought up to London by the Great Western
In a rather larger coffin
And driven slowly, oh so slowly

To the family burial ground at Esher
With all the relatives driving behind
Wearing black black black and peering furtively out of the
    carriage windows
To note for a moment that life was going on as usual.
For Aunt Cordelia was no symbol really
And her small death was of little account.
She was, after all, very old indeed
Although not quite so old as Queen Victoria
But on the other hand she didn't have so much prestige
Except of course in her own personal mind
And that was snuffed out at the same moment as everything
    else.
Also, unlike Queen Victoria, she had few mourners
Just the family and Mrs. Stokes who had been fond of her
And Miss Esme Banks who had looked after her in Torquay
And two remote cousins
Who couldn't rightly be classed as family
Because they were so very far removed
And only came to the cemetery because it was a sign of
    respect,
Respect, what is more, without hope
For there was little or no likelihood of their being mentioned
    in the will
But there they were all the same
Both tall and bent, in black toques with veils,
And both crying.

When Queen Victoria died
And was buried and the gun-carriage was dragged empty away
    again
The shops re-opened and so did the theatres
Although business was none too good.
But still it improved after a while
And everyone began to make plans for the Coronation
And it looked as if nothing much had happened

[73]

And perhaps nothing much had really
Except that an era, an epoch, an attitude of mind, was ended.

There would be other eras and epochs and attitudes of mind.
But never quite the same.

LETTER FROM THE SEASIDE (1880)

Dearest Mama
Here we all are
Safely arrived, with everything unpacked
Excepting the pilgrim basket and Laura's box
Which we are leaving until after tea
Because we want to go down to the sea
And look for seaweed and limpets on the rocks
And walk along the sands towards the caves
On the very edge of the waves.
We had, on the whole, a most agreeable journey
But for the fact
That poor Belinda
(Everything always happens to Belinda)
Got something in her eye, a piece of cinder.
You can imagine the relief
When Nanny cleverly managed to extract
The sharp invader with her handkerchief.
The name of our landlady is Mrs. Gurney.

Later. After tea.
Dearest Mama how glad, how proud you'll be
Arnold has paddled twice!
At first he was frightened and sat down and cried
On that hard kind of sand that's wrinkled by the tide
Until Nanny produced a piece of coconut-ice
Which we had bought in a shop on the Parade.
Soon his tears were dried, then suddenly, unafraid

Away he went, brave as a lion
Upheld on each side
By Belinda and Bryan
A tiny epitome of "Hearts of Oak"
Kicking the little wavelets as they broke!
For tea we had shrimps and cake and bread and butter
And they were pink, the shrimps I mean, bright pink
Can you imagine what Aunt Knox would think?
Can you not hear the prophecies she'd utter?
Her disapproving tone, her fearful warning
That we should all be dead before the morning!

These lodgings are very comfortable
Though we haven't yet tried the beds
Belinda and Laura are in the front
With a lithograph of Cain and Abel
And "The Light of the World" by Holman Hunt
Hanging above their heads.

Nanny's bedroom, which Arnold shares
Is across the landing and down three stairs.
Bryan and I have two small rooms
On the very topmost floor.
His is in front and mine's at the back
And a picture faces my door
Which someone cut out of an almanac
A picture of dashing young Hussars
Galloping off to war.
On the chest of drawers by the looking glass
There is—Imagine!—dried Pampas grass
Waving its fusty, dusty plumes
From a yellow Japanese vase.
But I can see over the sleeping town
To the curving line of the Sussex Down
And the sky and the moon and the stars.

Dearest Mama
Here we all are
Missing you so and wishing you could share
This pleasant gaslit room and the bracing air
And the prospect of tomorrow
For we are going on a picnic to a little bay
Beyond the lighthouse, several miles away.
Nanny has arranged with a Mr. Wells
To drive us in his wagonette
(Unless, of course, it's wet)
And Mrs. Gurney says that we can borrow
A wicker basket that she has, with handles,
In which to put the shells
And coloured pebbles that we hope to find on the deserted
    shore
Because, it seems, this particular beach
Is out of reach
Of ordinary visitors and is therefore lonely.
Oh dearest Mama—if only—if only
You could be here with us. Now I must close
This untidy, rambling letter
For Nanny has come in with our bedroom candles.
We all of us pray Papa will soon be better
And that tomorrow's weather will be fine.
Your loving and devoted—Caroline.

OPERA NOTES

I feel inclined to send a teeny-weeny
Admonishment to dear Signor Bellini
For having seriously tried to form a
Coherent opera from *Norma*.

I think we must face the fact that *Carmen* by Bizet
Is no more Spanish than the Champs Elysées.

Should I desire to be driven mad
I'd book a seat for *Herodiade*
Which, although it's by Massenet who wrote *Manon*
Is really not a good thing to plan on
And gives me by and large, more claust-
rophobia than *Faust*.

I often say, for which opera lovers attack me,
That if I were a soprano I'd let them sack me
Before I'd sing *Lakme*.

Nobody sane could bear to read a
Detailed synopsis of *Aida*
And we all know the plot of *La Gioconda*
Is apt to wander.
But neither of these so arch and sticky is
As *Gianni Schicchi* is.

Though Wolfgang Mozart wrote *The Magic Flute* he
Also, alas, composed *Cosi Fan Tutte*
The roguishness of which is piu piu male
Than *Don Pasquale*
But then poor Donizetti
Was likewise not
Too hot
At choosing Libretti.

Then there are those *Rosenkavaliers* and *Fledermauses*
Written by all those Strausses
Which play to crowded houses
And, to me, are louses.

There couldn't be a sillier story
Than *Il Trovatore*
And yet, and yet, and yet Oh
Just think of the libretto
Of *Rigoletto!*
Both of these were set to music by Verdi
How dared he?
On the other hand we must admit that *Thaïs*
Is more concaïs
And fairly naïs

We must also admit that every Victorian Hurdy-gurdy
Owes a deep debt of gratitude to Giuseppe Verdi.

MORNING GLORY

"There's something rather sad," she said
"In seeing a great big ship go down"
She languidly shook her lovely head
And plucked the edge of the eiderdown.
Her hands were white and her nails were red
Her marble brow wore a pensive frown
"It's really terribly sad," she said
"To see a beautiful ship go down."
The breakfast tray lay across her knee
A dusty beam of sunlight shone
On fruit and silver and China tea
And a crumbled, half-devoured scone.
The thin blue smoke of her cigarette
Wove, above us, a tangled skein,
The end of it, where her lips had met,
Proudly boasted a scarlet stain.
As though appalled by her own surmise
She gave a shudder and then a stretch
And turned her empty, lambent eyes
To have a look at the Daily Sketch.
The front page headlines were large and black
The pictures under them blotched, obscene
A few dark heads in the swirling wrack
"Survivors stories on page sixteen"
She read a little and sipped her tea
"Fifty passengers safe and sound"
Then she brightened perceptibly

"Fourteen hundred and fifty drowned"
She read the glutinous journalese
That smeared the names of the lost and dead
Then, rather neatly, controlled a sneeze
"That was sheer agony," she said
I looked at the lissom, graceful line
Her body made 'neath the silken sheet
Her heart so far so far from mine
Yet I could almost hear it beat.
I wandered back over hours of sleep
To try to catch at the night gone by
To see if morning would let me keep
At least a fragment of memory.

THE BATTLE OF BRITAIN DINNER
NEW YORK, 1963

I have been to the "Battle of Britain" dinner.
Held at the Hotel Shelbourne on 37th street and Lexington
And there they were, a few survivors
Of that long dead victory
And there they were too, the non-survivors
Somewhere in the air above us,
Or at any rate in our hearts
The young men who died, humorously, gaily, making jokes
Until the moment when swift blazing death annihilated them.
And there we were, raising our glasses to them
Drinking to their intolerable gallantry
And trying to make believe that their sacrifice
Was worth while
Perhaps it was worth while for them, but not for us.
They flew out of life triumphant, leaving us to see
The ideal that they died for humiliated and betrayed
Even more than it had been betrayed at Munich
By those conceited, foolish, frightened old men.
Today in our country it is the young men who are frightened
They write shrill plays about defeat and are hailed as
        progressive
They disdain our great heritage. They have been labelled by
        their dull
Facile contemporaries as "Angry Young Men"
But they are not angry, merely scared and ignorant.
Many of them are not even English
But humourless refugees from alien lands

Seeking protection in our English sanity
And spitting on the valiant centuries
That made the sanity possible.
These clever ones, these terrified young men
Who so fear extinction and the Atom bomb
Have little in common with the men we were remembering
    tonight
Whatever fears they had remained unspoken. They flew daily and
    nightly into the sky
Heavily outnumbered by the enemy and saved us for one
    valedictory year
Gave us one last great chance
To prove to a bemused and muddled world
Our basic quality. All that was done.
The year was lived alone and then
Conveniently forgotten and dismissed
Except for just one night in each long year.
We raised our glasses sentimentally
An Air Vice Marshal made a brief, appropriate speech
And then we chatted a little, oppressed by anti-climax
And finally said goodnight and went our ways.

IRENE VANBRUGH MEMORIAL MATINEE
THE EPILOGUE

Your Majesty, Ladies and Gentlemen.
A little while ago a lady died
A lady who, for many of us here
Epitomised the dignity and pride
Of our profession. Over fifty years
Have passed since young Miss Vanbrugh's quality
Was stamped indelibly upon the hearts
Of Londoners. During those changing years
We were most privileged, not only us
Her colleagues who so loved and honoured her
But you as well, you on the other side.
Perhaps you took for granted (as you should)
The lightness of her touch in comedy;
The note of hidden laughter in her voice;
The way she used her hands to illustrate
Some subtle implication. She could charge
An ordinary line with so much wit
That even critics thought the play was good!
They too, took her for granted (as they should).
Then on the other hand, the other mask,
The mask of tragedy; she could wear that
With such authority that even we,
Her fellow actors plainly could perceive
Through her most accurate and sure technique
Her truth, which was her talent, shining clear.
Your Majesty, Ladies and Gentlemen,
A little while ago this lady died

Apparently, only apparently,
For even though the art that she adorned
Must in its essence be ephemeral,
Players of her integrity and grace
Can never die. Although we shall not hear
That lyrical, gay voice again, nor see
The personal inimitable smile
That she bestowed on us at curtain calls
The theatre that she loved will still go on
Enriched immeasurably by the years
She gave to it. This epilogue is but
A prelude to the future she endowed
With so much legend, so much memory
For all the young beginners who will learn
Their intricate and fascinating trade
And owe perhaps, some measure of their fame
To the undying magic of her name.

NOT YET THE DODO

In the countryside of England
Tucked snugly beneath the Sussex Downs
Or perhaps a mile or two away
From gentle cathedral towns
There still exist today
A diminishing few
A residue
Of unregenerate characters who
Despite two wars and the Welfare State
And incomes sadly inadequate
Still, summoned by Sunday morning chimes,
Walk briskly to church to say their prayers
And later, in faded chintz arm-chairs,
Read of divorces, wars and crimes
And, shocked by the trend of world affairs,
Compose,
In a cosy, post-prandial doze,
Tart letters of protest to *The Times*.
These people still tap the weather-glass
And prune their roses and mow their grass
Representative
For so long as they live
Of the English upper middle-class.

General and Lady Bedrington
Lived on the borders of Cornwall and Devon
In a red-brick, weather-bleached Georgian house

With a distant view of the sea,
They drove into Plymouth twice a week
In an ancient Austin Seven
And in summer, on rather a sloping lawn,
Played croquet after tea,
The thirty years of their married life
Had been lived in far away places,
Before and during and after the war
They'd always been on the move.
Alien climates and tropical suns
Had sallowed their English faces
And now, at long last, their elderly ways
Were set in a tranquil groove.
The household staff which should have been six
Was reduced to one and a "Daily."
The "One" was Maggie Macdonald
Who'd been Lady Bedrington's maid
In the early, hurly-burly days
When they'd settled themselves so gaily
In that "Barracky" house in the compound
Of the Garrison at Port Said.
Later, when Priscilla was born
And so sadly and swiftly died,
It was Maggie who coped with everything,
Efficient beyond belief.
It was Maggie who, in the desolate hours,
Stayed by her mistress's side
And with dour, stubborn Scottish sense,
Blunted the edges of grief.

It was Maggie also who, some years after,
When Barry was born in Delhi,
Nursed Lady B through the merciless heat
And ultimately contrived,
On a breathless morning at six o'clock,
While the bugles were sounding Reveille,

To deliver the baby an hour and a half
Before the doctor arrived.
And later still, when war had come,
She brought the boy home to his Granny
In a crowded troopship that sailed for England
Under a brazen sky.
She fluttered a handkerchief from the deck,
Proud of her role as a Nanny,
While Lady Bedrington, blinded with tears,
Waved the convoy good-bye.

Maggie Macdonald was old and grey
But far from full of sleep
She had rheumatism in hip and knee
And her eyes were not what they used to be
But she woke with the morning every day
As though she'd a tryst to keep.

She ran the house like an oiled machine,
She did the marketing, cooked the meals:
On afternoons off, in her Sunday black
She walked three miles to the village and back
With a vast, asthmatical Aberdeen
Lumbering at her heels.

Maggie saw no indignity
In the fact that she worked for others.
She returned to Scotland once a year
For a fortnight's family atmosphere
In a little grey house outside Dundee
With one of her married brothers.

There were lots of relatives, brusque but kind;
Grandnephews and nieces to see
She brought them presents and gave them treats
And walked with them through the Dundee streets
But always, at the back of her mind,
Were the General and Lady B.

But even more than the Bedringtons
It was Barry who claimed her heart,
She wept each time he left for school,
Upbraiding herself for a doting fool
And stuffed him with cream and saffron buns
And apple and blackberry tart.

And when, as an undergraduate,
He came home for long week-ends,
She washed his shirts and pressed his slacks
And lied for him and covered his tracks
And was ready with soda-bicarbonate
For him and his Oxford friends.

The problem of Barry's future career
Blew up at his coming-of-age.
He chose his moment and seized his chance
And, in the library after the dance
Announced, in a voice quite firm and clear,
That he meant to go on the stage.

The General went purple in the face,
Lady Bedrington kept her head.
They both of them tried to talk him round
But the boy inflexibly held his ground
Until at last, with unhappy grace,
They surrendered and went to bed.

Maggie was told the news the next day
And felt she might easily faint
But she pursed her lips and packed his bags,
Gloomily tied on the luggage tags
And waved the pride of her life away
To his world of powder and paint.

General and Lady Bedrington
With inward excitement but outward calm
Arrived, as usual, at Paddington
Where Barry was awaiting, efficient and kind,
Though the General noticed, with vague alarm,
That his hair was rather too long behind.
With him was standing a tall young man
Wearing corduroys and an open sweater
Who, Barry explained, was Danny Hoag
With whom he was sharing a two-room flat
In a cul-de-sac off the Earl's Court Road.
He added, impressively, that Dan
Quite frequently drew designs for Vogue
And Lady B, with a private sigh,
Ardently wished she could like him better.
Barry procured a cab outside
And off they drove through the London rain
Danny dripping with Irish charm,
Caressing them with his gentle brogue
Barry, voluble, chatting away,
Telling them with self-conscious pride,
About the theatre, about the play,
About some pompous old Blimp who wrote
Explosively to the Telegraph
Protesting against the author's use
Of four-letter words and his abuse
Of England's quality, England's pride
England's achievements past and present.

The General stared at the street outside
And thought the play sounded damned unpleasant.

When they had reached the De Glenn hotel
And the boys had taken the taxi on,
General and Lady Bedrington,
After their welcome from the staff,
Walked upstairs to their double room
Both thinking thoughts best left unsaid
Both of them trying valiantly,
Sitting together on the bed,
To help each other to vanquish gloom.
"I didn't think much of that Irish bloke!"
The General murmured unhappily.
His wife, as though he had made a joke,
Laughed indulgently, patted his knee
And telephoned down to order tea.

They went to the theatre
Sat through the play
And were shocked, bewildered and bored,
And during the final curtain calls,
Numb, in their complimentary stalls,
They looked at each other, looked away
And forced themselves to applaud.

The audience straggled up the aisle
And vanished into the Mews
But both the General and Lady B,
Frozen in hopeless apathy
Sat on in silence for a while
Like people who've had bad news.

Stunned, inarticulate and deeply tired
They finally were led resignedly
Up four steep steps and through an iron door

To meet the cast and author of the play.
The odd young woman who escorted them
Wore, with a skin-tight jumper, denim slacks,
Black stockings, grubby plimsoles and a beret
From under which curtains of greasy hair
Descended to her shoulders. On the stage
Barry received them and presented them
With filial pride and touching eagerness,
To all his strange colleagues who stood around
Proudly upon their consecrated ground.
Poor Lady Bedrington, with social grace,
Managed to conquer her embarrassment
And murmur some polite but empty phrases.
The General, mute before his only son,
Finally cleared his throat and said, "Well done!"

The supper party after the play
In Barry and Danny's flat
Could not be accurately dubbed
An unqualified success.
The cast were all invited
And some other cronies appeared
Including a sibilant gentleman
In velvet slacks and a beard
And a sullen Lesbian in evening dress
Who brought a Siamese cat.

General and Lady B were received
With cautious politesse
A tall girl offered them sandwiches
And a whisky and soda each.
They sat on a sofa side by side
And longed to be home in bed.
There was little ham in the sandwiches
And a great deal too much bread

But they chewed them bravely, bereft of speech,
Encased in self-consciousness.

The party, after an hour or two,
Abandoned its formal endeavour.
A sallow youth with enormous ears
Was coaxed to do imitations.
The people he mimic'd obviously
Were known to everyone there
But the Bedringtons rather missed the point
For they didn't know who they were
And Barry's hissed explanations
Bewildered them more than ever.

A girl with slightly projecting teeth
Agreed, after much persuasion,
To tell the story of how she'd been
Seduced in "digs" in Hull.
The present company evidently
Had heard it often before
And when she'd finished, vociferously,
Demanded an encore
To which she at once assented
And told an equally dull,
Long, complicated anecdote
Which was even more Rabelaisian.

The Bedringtons, over their married years,
Had learned to accept defeats.
So, at the same moment, they both got up
Still smiling with frozen eyes.
A hush descended upon the group
While politenesses were said
And Lady Bedrington's cloak was fetched
From Barry and Danny's bed.
Barry got them a taxi

And, muttering swift good-byes
They drove back to the De Glenn hotel
Through the bright, deserted streets.

That night they lay, restless, in their thin twin beds
And Lady B discreetly wept a little.
The General, equally wretched, bravely tried
To reassure her, soothe her with platitudes.
"Youth will be served," he said, "We can't expect
Old heads on young shoulders, this is a passing phase,
He'll soon grow out of it. Cheer up my dear,
It's dangerous to take up moral attitudes.
Let the young idiot and his ghastly friends
Enjoy themselves and go their foolish ways."
He got out of his bed to kiss her cheek
As he had done for nearly forty years.
"Silly old thing," she said, and dried her tears.
The General, having got back into bed,
Switched off the light and, turning on his side,
Tried, unsuccessfully, to sleep.
Lady B also, in the oppressive dark,
Waited unhopefully for oblivion.
Again, entirely soundlessly, she wept
And it was almost dawn before they slept.

To Royal garden parties every year
Vast numbers of loyal subjects are invited.
From South and West and East and North they come,
Some from the country, some from the suburbs, some
(On leave from Zanzibar or the Seychelles)
From inexpensive Kensington hotels.
Matriarchs in large hats and flowered prints,
Ebony delegates from far Dominions,
One or two sharp-eyed ladies from the Press,
Tiny green gentlemen in native dress,
Colonial Governors with eager wives

Jostling in line for when the Queen arrives.
Bright Debutantes quite recently presented,
Actresses of impeccable repute,
A novelist or two, Bishops galore,
Plus members of the Diplomatic corps,
A smattering of ancient Admirals
And matrons from the London hospitals.
Cabinet ministers, some rural Deans,
Newly created Knights and Peers and Dames,
Field Marshals, Air Marshals, a few V.C.'s.
Sauntering beneath the Royal trees
Every mutation of the middle-class
Proudly parading on the Royal grass.
The Queen, surrounded by her retinue,
Graciously moves among her varied guests.
Curtseys are made, heads are correctly bowed
And as she makes her progress through the crowd
Pauses are organised for conversation
With those marked on the list for presentation.
Following her, forming their separate groups,
Come other members of the Royal family.
Sharing with affable, polite mobility,
Part of the afternoon's responsibility.
After an hour or so of this routine,
Either in blazing sun or gentle rain,
The Royalties, by mutual consent,
Withdraw themselves to an exclusive tent,
Weary of bobbing head and bended knee,
And thankfully sit down to have their tea.

The porter at the De Glenn hotel
Having procured a hired limousine,
Stood to attention as the Bedringtons
Set proudly forth to keep their Regal tryst.
The General, in top hat and morning coat,
Lady B, in a floating chiffon dress,

Climbed with unhurried calm into the car
Though Lady B's enormous cartwheel hat
Needed to be manoeuvred with some care.
Walter, the valet, Rose, the chambermaid,
Ernest, the waiter on the second floor,
Waved from the landing window, while Miss Holt,
Her pince-nez glinting in the morning sun,
Forsook the cashier's desk and with a cry,
Rushed down the hotel steps to say good-bye.

We British are a peculiar breed
Undemonstrative on the whole.
It takes a very big shock indeed
To dent our maddening self-control.

The slow decline of our Island Race
Alien prophets have long foreseen,
But still, to symbolise English grace,
We go to London to see the Queen.

Our far-flung Empire imposed new rules
And lasted a century or so
Until, engrossed with our Football Pools
We shrugged our shoulders and let it go.

But old traditions are hard to kill
However battered about they've been.
And it's still, for some, an authentic thrill
To go to London to see the Queen.

The car moved very slowly through the traffic.
Its occupants sat still, preserving elegance,
The General would have liked to cross his legs
And smoke a cigarette, but he refrained;
His trousers were well-pressed and must remain
Well-pressed until he got back home again.

Sense of Occasion and the Royal touch
Wakened in their reactionary hearts
Old memories of less disturbing years
When social values were more specified.
Before the Proletariat, en masse,
Reversed the status of the ruling class.

For them the afternoon (until the end)
Was beautiful and somehow reassuring.
They saw the Queen pass by and Lady B
Executed a most successful curtsey:
Then the Queen Mother, with her lovely smile,
Chatted to them both for quite a while.

Past friends appeared, perhaps a little changed:
Emily Blake who'd made that awful scene
With Boy Macfadden on the Polo ground;
Both of the Granger girls, now safely married,
Isabel Pratt, whose face had grown much larger,
Still with her rather dubious Maharajah.

The Hodgsons, alas, in mourning for poor Hilda;
Vernon and Hattie Phillips from Madras,
Everyone welcoming, everyone pleased to see them,
But typically it was Ella Graves
Wearing a hideous hat and sharp with malice,
Who pounced upon them as they left the Palace.

Eleanor Graves, née Eleanor Walker,
Had always been a compulsive talker,
A fact
Which, combined with her monumental lack of tact,
Caused quite a lot of people to avoid her.
This might conceivably have annoyed her
Very much indeed
If she'd

Possessed enough humility to perceive it,
Or believe it,
But Oh no—Oh dear me no!
Her sense of superiority was so
Deeply ingrained
That she remained
Garrulous, mischievous and indiscreet,
Blandly protected by her own conceit.
"I'd no idea you were here!" she shrieked,
Inserting herself between them,
And "It seemed like centuries" she wailed,
"Since the last time she'd seen them."
She said they *must* see her sweet new flat,
"Just pop in for drinks, or dine"
And added, with shrill irrelevance,
That Lady B's hat was divine.
They were trapped there, waiting for their car
Without a hope of escape.
The General wished she could be tied up
And gagged with adhesive tape.
It wasn't until they'd both agreed
To lunch on the following day
That at long long last their car appeared
And they thankfully drove away.

It was after lunch on the next unhappy day,
When her other guests had said their good-byes and left,
That Eleanor, insufferably mysterious,
Seized on the moment she'd been waiting for.
"There's something I just must warn you about," she hissed,
"And if you weren't such old and valued friends,
I wouldn't interfere or say a word,
But as I'm so fond of you and this is serious,
I thought I'd take my courage in both hands
And tell you, straight from the shoulder, what I've heard
About your Barry and that Irish character

Who, judging from all accounts, are quite inseparable.
As yet the situation's not irreparable,
But action must be taken, something done,
To salvage the reputation of your son."

The General's eyes became cold and bleak.
He set his jaw and his face was grim.
He opened his mouth, prepared to speak,
But Lady B was too quick for him.
She rose to her feet and swiftly turned
With smiling lips and a heart of lead.
"How kind of you to be so concerned,
We're both devoted to Dan," she said.

On leaving Eleanor's flat they took a bus
And sat in silence, worried and unhappy.
They left the bus at Prince's Gate and walked
Into the Park, still without speaking, still
Struggling to evade the implications
Of Eleanor's malign insinuations.

Sitting on two green chairs beneath the trees
They absently surveyed the London Pastoral:
Nurses and children, governesses, dogs,
Two lovers sleeping in each other's arms,
A young man with his coloured shirt undone
Profiting from the unexpected sun.

Mutely they realised that here and now
It was essential for them both to face
Some of the facts of life which, hitherto,
Their inbred reticence had stowed away,
With other fixed taboos of various kinds,
Down in the depths of their subconscious minds.

Their self-protective innocence of course
Was not as valid as it seemed to be.
They both of them, within their private thoughts,
Knew things that neither of them would admit.
Lady B traced patterns on the ground,
With her umbrella tip. The General frowned.

Sitting there quietly on their painted chairs
Aware that they were together, yet alone,
They watched, without noticing, the changing scene:
The brilliant sunlight of the afternoon
Softening and merging into early evening
The shadows lengthening under the London trees,
Staining with grey the brownish, trodden grass.
The summer noises seemed to be changing too
Becoming less strident as the day wore on:
The hum of traffic, buses grinding gears,
Children's shrill voices, sharp staccato barks
From those alert, exclusively London dogs
Which seem indigenous to London Parks.
Finally, stiffly, they got up and walked,
Still without speaking, back to the hotel.
In both their minds decisions had been made,
Mutually arrived at, without discussion,
And when they reached their bedroom Lady B
Took off her hat, stared in the looking glass
And searched her face with anxious scrutiny
Discovering with relief that all the strains
And inward conflicts of the last few hours
Had left no outward traces to betray her.
Her eyes perhaps did look a trifle tired
But then, all things considered, that was not
Entirely to be wondered at. She sat
Decisively upon the bed and took
The telephone receiver from its hook.

Barry and Danny got back to the flat at six
After a rather aimless afternoon
Searching for antiques in the Brompton road.
Barry was hot, irritable, conscious of guilt,
Because he hadn't made the slightest effort
To find out if his parents were all right
And if their glum little Kensington hotel
Was comfortable. He could have sent some flowers
If he had thought of it. He mooched about,
Took off his clothes and flung himself on the bed.
Danny looked at him quizzically and said,
"Why don't we call your rather frightening mother
And ask them both to dine somewhere or other?"

The telephone, at that moment, rang.
Barry lifted it to his ear
And suffered a further guilty pang
When his mother's voice said, "Is that you dear?"

At any rate the evening went off well.
The Bedringtons were fetched from their hotel,
Squeezed into Danny's second-hand M.G.
And driven, perhaps a thought erratically,
To dine in a converted Wesleyan chapel
Called, rather whimsically, "The Golden Apple."

The room was tiny, lit by flickering candles.
The waiters wore canvas trousers, vests and sandals,
The menus, although very large indeed,
The General found difficult to read,
Poor Lady B in her self-conscious flurry
Rather unwisely plumped for chicken curry.

The noise was deafening, the service, slow.
Danny, resolved to make the party go,
Laid himself out, with Irish charm and wit,
To loosen up the atmosphere a bit.
And Lady B was vaguely mortified
To see the General laugh until he cried.

Later that evening, General and Lady B,
Preoccupied with their eventful day,
Slowly prepared themselves to face the night.
Lady B pensively took off her rings
And put them in the dressing-table drawer.
The General went stumping down the passage
As usual, to the bathroom, with his sponge bag.
Lady B rubbing her face with cleansing cream,
Could hear him in the distance, gargling.
Suddenly she remembered Ella's words:
Her bland, unwarranted impertinence,
"That Irish character" "Something must be done"
"To save the reputation of your son!"
Lady B conscious that her hands were shaking,
Made a tremendous effort at control
And, with a slight, contemptuous grimace,
Firmly continued massaging her face.

On the fourth day of their dejected holiday,
Breakfasting in the hotel dining room,
General and Lady B, without discussion,
Inspired by age-old mutual telepathy,
Arrived at the same conclusion. Lady B
Absently took some toast, then put it back.
"I think" she said, "I'll go upstairs and pack."

It was Danny who answered the telephone,
Barry was still asleep.
Lady B's voice was icily polite,

"I really must apologise" she said
"For calling you so early in the morning.
I'd like to have a few words with my son
However if he isn't yet awake
Please don't disturb him—You could perhaps explain,
We've had a tiresome telegram from home
Which means that we must leave immediately
And so we are leaving on the mid-day train."
Danny, completely taken by surprise,
Tried, unsuccessfully, to sound dismayed
But Lady B cut short his protestations
Quite firmly, still implacably polite.
"Please tell him" she went on, "That we will write
The moment we get back. It *was* such fun"
She added "Dining with you both
At that strange restaurant the other night."

Maggie Macdonald had second sight
A loving, instinctive flair.
The telegram Lady B had sent
Confirmed her growing presentiment
That trouble was in the air.

She waited grimly to meet the train
Though her welcoming smile was gay
And while they greeted her normally
And chatted away informally
She searched their faces for signs of strain
And the signs were as clear as day.

At dinner, outwardly serene,
The General praised the salmon.
Afterwards he and Lady B
Sat for a while and watched TV
Then, gallantly loyal to routine,
Played three games of Backgammon.

[103]

Maggie, knowing her mistress very well
Was certain she would not go up to bed
Without some hint, some sort of explanation
Of why they had so suddenly returned.
So, busying herself with little chores,
She put the cat out, tidied the dresser drawers,
Ironed some handkerchiefs and wound the clock,
Pottered about, arranged the breakfast tray,
Put on the kettle for a cup of tea
And finally, with nothing else to do,
She sat down in her creaking cane arm-chair
And waited for a footstep on the stair.
She heard the front door slam and knew the General
Had gone out for his customary stroll;
Silence enclosed the house, silence so deep
That the bland ticking of the kitchen clock
Sounded presumptuous, a loud intrusion,
Confusing more her heart's dismayed confusion.
Edward miaowed outside, she let him in
And, stalking before her like a conqueror,
He jumped into his basket, washed his face,
Shot her a glance and delicately yawned.
She gently massaged him behind the ears
And, unaccountably, burst into tears.

Of course, at this moment, Lady B appeared
Catching poor Maggie red-eyed and betrayed.
She paused for a moment at the door and then
Swiftly advanced and took her in her arms.
"Don't Maggie dear, please please don't cry" she said
"It isn't all that bad, really it's not.
Nothing appalling's happened, nothing sad,
Merely a tiresomeness, let's just sit down
Quite calmly and discuss it, you and me,
And, while we're at it, have a cup of tea."

[104]

They sat there in close conference
With their crowded years behind them
Both bewildered and both distressed
But both determined to do their best
Not to allow their innocence
And prejudices to blind them.

They both knew more and they both knew less
Than either of them admitted.
To them, the infinite, complex
And strange divergencies of sex
Were based on moral capriciousness
And less to be blamed than pitied.

They both agreed that there'd always seemed
A "difference" about Barry.
He'd never plagued them with sudden scares
Involving dubious love affairs;
Preserving himself, so they fondly dreamed,
For the girl he would finally marry.

But here they were guilty of sophistry
For, with deep, unspoken dread,
Their minds rejected the ghastly day
That would whisk their paragon away
Beyond their possessive idolatry
To an alien marriage bed.

Their earlier fears having been replaced
By faintly embarrassed relief,
They tried, with mutual urgency,
To cope with this new emergency;
Like storm-tossed mariners suddenly faced
With a strange, uncharted reef.

For more than three hours they sat there in the kitchen.
Maggie made sandwiches and brewed fresh tea.
Out in the quiet night the world was sleeping
Lulled by the murmur of the distant sea.
Finally Maggie, with shrewd common sense,
Embarked upon her speech for the defence.

"If you want my opinion" she said, "I think
We're both of us wasting our breath.
You can't judge people by rule of thumb
And if we sit gabbing till Kingdom Come
We'll neither one of us sleep a wink
And worry ourselves to death.

People are made the way they're made
And it isn't anyone's fault.
Nobody's tastes can quite agree,
Some like coffee and some like tea
And Guinness rather than lemonade
And pepper rather than salt.

If Mr. Barry had got caught out
By some little teenage whore
And brought her home as his blushing bride
Not only would we be mortified,
But we'd have a real problem to fuss about
And worry a great deal more.

Being a 'spinster' as you might say
Not overburdened with looks,
I never went in for much romance
Though I had some fun when I got the chance
And whatever knowledge has come my way
Has come through people and books.

I don't know what this is all about
But Barry's the one I care for.
I don't mind whether he's strange or not
Or goes to bed with a Hottentot.
It's no good us trying to puzzle out
The what, the why and the wherefore."

When Maggie's tirade came to an end
She suddenly bowed her head.
Lady B rose and kissed her cheek
And, when she could trust herself to speak
Said "Now, my most loyal and loving friend
It's time we went up to bed."

During the next few days the weather held.
The russet Devon cliffs cast purple shadows
Staining the edges of the quiet sea.
The General played golf, Lady B pottered
About the garden, old Mrs. Macklehenny
Drove out from Saltash with her married niece,
Ate a vast luncheon and remained for tea.
On the fifth morning Lady B sat down
Purposefully at her writing desk,
Unscrewed her fountain pen, stared at the view,
Absently noting an old cargo ship
Lumbering across the shining bay.
The dark smoke from its funnel twisting high
Scribbled a question mark against the sky.
"My darling boy" she wrote, "You really must
Forgive me for not writing days ago
To thank you for our little jaunt to Town.
You can't imagine how Papa and I
Enjoyed ourselves, you really were so sweet
To give your aged parents such a treat.
The weather here is perfect, not a cloud.

You'd almost think you were in Italy.
The garden's drying up of course, no rain
For nearly two whole weeks. Old Mr. Drew,
The one who used to help you with your stamps,
Suddenly died last Saturday, so sad
But still, all things considered, a release,
When one is ninety-four one can't complain
At ceasing upon the midnight with no pain.
The Hilliard girls are back from Switzerland
Looking, Papa says, commoner than ever.
Hilda, the one who's said to be so clever,
Met some professor in the Engadine
And got engaged to him all in a minute!
As he's apparently quite mad and drinks
Perhaps she's not so clever as she thinks.
That's all my news and so I'd better stop
And not go rambling on like poor Aunt Jane
Who, incidentally, fell down again
Just outside Gorringe's, the poor old duck
Seems to be really haunted by bad luck."
Lady B paused, and, nibbling at her pen,
Frowned for a moment and then wrote "P.S.
Please give our love to Danny and remember
That we expect you *both* in mid-September."

General and Lady Bedrington
Lived on the borders of Cornwall and Devon
In a red-brick, weather-bleached Georgian house
With its distant view of the sea.
They still drove to Plymouth twice a week
In their rattling Austin Seven
And still, if the weather was feasible,
Played croquet after tea.

Maggie still tramped to the village
With Black Angus, the Aberdeen.
The sun still rose and the sun still set
And the Eddystone light still shone.
Lady B and the General both
Encased in their daily routine
Began insensibly to forget
Their excursion to Babylon.